Serene

Poetry by
Evan Quitelle

Order this book online at www.trafford.com
or email orders@trafford.com

Most Trafford titles are also available at major online book retailers.

© Copyright 2018 Evan Quitelle.
All rights reserved. No part of this publication may be reproduced, stored in a retrieval system, or transmitted, in any form or by any means, electronic, mechanical, photocopying, recording, or otherwise, without the written prior permission of the author.

Print information available on the last page.

ISBN: 978-1-4907-8944-6 (sc)
ISBN: 978-1-4907-8943-9 (hc)
ISBN: 978-1-4907-8945-3 (e)

Library of Congress Control Number: 2018948059

Because of the dynamic nature of the Internet, any web addresses or links contained in this book may have changed since publication and may no longer be valid. The views expressed in this work are solely those of the author and do not necessarily reflect the views of the publisher, and the publisher hereby disclaims any responsibility for them.

Any people depicted in stock imagery provided by Getty Images are models, and such images are being used for illustrative purposes only.
Certain stock imagery © Getty Images.

Trafford rev. 06/15/2018

www.trafford.com

North America & international
toll-free: 1 888 232 4444 (USA & Canada)
fax: 812 355 4082

Contents

This Book Is Dedicated To My Wife On Our Wedding Day

SEVAN 13 18

Serene I Love You

Acknowledgements

Team SEVAN 13 Serene, Evan, Qari, Lateef, Arianna, Briel and Mason

Chartreuse With Envy

Upon your entrance
there is light from
the angles of your beauty
and the audience has
become dear in the light
there are many in the
kaleidoscope that dream
of being the light
yet while you have them
distracted there are plots
to steal away the silver spoon
that is your birthright

She Breathes Fire

She has killed
many men nesting
in their egos

Cremated most
while others have
drowned in the moat
that circumscribes her

There is venom in her kisses
from lips that taste of nectar
a sword her tongue cuts down to size
she is a warrior

Her landscape is divine
there is execution in her walk
she switches with a royal sashay
like hot lava honey flows from those hips

Made in his image
she is goddess

The Duchess of Lillibridge

On Lillibridge
that cat with the
Cadillac gave berth
to nine lives
heading for the
drive in theatre
stopping only to
fill up on root beer
floats at pump
number thirteen
and just like that
banana split
no phones to be
heard in the distance
no being tickled pink
no getting wet with sprinkles
on a pineapple Sunday
the Duchess was the youngest
of the litter

Sunflower

Who gave birth to this vision
to tell a thousand times I love

Who had the audacity in the
produce section to put her on the grid

Who covered her hair in
sunflower barrettes and placed

Her in a field of lilies to blossom
and to bloom

Who blessed her with the scent
sweeter than perfume and kissed

Her skin the color of almond
and honey for bees to consume

This girl raised in
Detroit

South For The Winter

Have you ever taken
off your halo and wings

Do you wash them on
gentle cycle and tumble

Dry or do they read dry
clean only when I hug you

Do I squeeze them too tight
they say we are inseparable

They say you're a bird of pray
a ministering angel I'm going

South for the winter can I take
you there and if birds of a

Feather flock together does
that make me an angel too

Sacred

Dying is not
above reproach

there is a fate
worse than death

to live in a world
that is not Serene

to be her accomplice
killing time

this goddess made
in his image

she is sacred

she is love and I
would lay down

my life for love

this angel not
sent from above

she is heaven

Anchored

I wonder if we fell
in love on the pier
that day we stood
there talking as sailors
left for liberty in
between reveille and
taps the skyscrapers
were giant grey ships
anchored no rotating
or radiating while men
were working aloft and
two souls were being
elevated was the
conversation about
dreams and had she at
that moment already
begun to anchor mine

Autumn From Heaven

There are leaves of absence falling from the sky
not sure why there was this sabbatical
plummeting down to walk among the hueless
vibrant and angelic taking pleasure in the fall
did she come for me like the reaper only not so grim
was this my savior cloaked in sage eyes and a veil of white
drawn to her with the gravitational force of attraction
I have been so anxious hoping for this occurrence to happen
the anticipation I have been preparing and now chivalry shall
be the best of me I have been waiting for this since before the
cocooning of manhood waiting for the fall for her to season
to flavor my existence giving me a glimpse of Heaven

The Beautiful Yawn

There is beauty
in the yawn it is contagious
catching like love nestled
in a keeping place safe and secure

there is a snoring
softly curled up next to me
peaceful it has relieved the yawn
yet still beautiful and gentle

I want to live
to take up residence

to stay here in this sanctuary

where the beautiful yawn

Dancing In The Serene Reign

I will not
take shelter
I came to
dance to the
rhythm of her
reign the
Serene before
the storm
I will take
refuge in it
to be royally
drenched in
her magnitude
when she pours
there's overflow
tranquility
amid the chaos

Anchored

I wonder if we fell
in love on the pier
that day we stood
there talking as sailors
left for liberty in
between reveille and
taps the skyscrapers
were giant grey ships
anchored no rotating
or radiating while men
were working aloft and
two souls were being
elevated was the
conversation about
dreams and had she at
that moment already
begun to anchor mine

Ring The Belle

I cannot live without
water I cannot live
without food for
nourishment
without the air that
I breathe and I cannot
live without you
you are autumn from
Heaven my angel you
are beautiful and I thank
God for you my best
friend I am blessed I get
to wake up beside Heaven
every morning while most
men dream of being rich
and famous doctors and
lawyers or the president of
the United States my dreams
were of you. I have waited
for this moment all of my
life and now
I promise to leave
the toilet seat down.
let you control the
remote. let the paper
roll in the direction
of your choosing.
change the light
bulbs over the mirror
in the bathrooms.
leave the heat on 72.
wash the dishes and
even do a load of
laundry every now and
then. put out the trash.

I will only put the vacuum
cleaner down when it is
time to put away the groceries.
scratch your back, massage your feet
run your bath water
fill your car with gas
cook dinner on my night
I promise to laugh at
your jokes. bring your
favorite flowers and
See's candy on date
night. shoulder the
weight of it all. profess,
protect, provide, cherish,
shelter, be a refuge. you
are my Ruth
if someone says to you
I hear him professing and
he looks to have the
strength to be a protector
but can he keep a roof
over your head is he
a provider? you can say
with confidence in his
father's house there
are many mansions.
if someone asks you
why is your husband's
knees so ashy you can
boldly say because he
stays on his knees praying
for me for us for our family
and if asked does he truly
love you unconditionally?
(hold up and point at your
ring finger) and say "upon
this rock he has built his church."
you are my temple, sanctuary,
my purpose my dwelling place
my strength my best friend
and I love you but loving you is

not enough. walking with you
worshiping with you adoring
edifying you and lifting you
up in prayer. at the altar
I am going to ring the belle.
in my Boaz voice "glean from
my field Ruth" this is our season.
just like Eve completed Adam in Eden
with you my life is Serene
you are my nourishment you quench my thirst
you are the heir that I breathe.

In The Near Distance

I am making
a spectacle
of myself
over the girl
in the Gucci
glasses with
the honey
brown eyes
and magnifying
beauty who left
me unbalanced
with a wink the
distance near a
future in focus
giving insight
doubling a single
point of view
I can see me
getting down
on one knee
my vision is to
altar her state

Motown Philly Love

When Smokey Robinson and his Miracles were blaring
"Cruisin" from my eight track and "Grease" was top of
the box office at the drive-in when Chief Jay Strongbow
came off the top turnbuckle when penny candy was still
a penny when I gave you a bite of my cheesesteak

I knew I loved you then

When you were paying me no never mind sippin' on your
Faygo pop and eating your Better Made Specials when
we still shopped at Woolworth's and Woolco and got our
hoagie from the delicatessen and our four chicken wings
with hot sauce for a dollar from the Lunch Box

I knew I loved you then

When sightseers took in the giant clothes pin and the giant Uniroyal
tire when someone scratched my Stylistics and Temptations
forty five when I gave you one third of my butterscotch krimpet
and half of my cream soda when I bought two soft pretzels

I knew I loved you then

Migration Of The Dear

Two box cars coupled
together in matrimony
one filled with baggage
the other precious cargo
dressed in a leisure pursuit
even coupled side by side
the distance is unbearable

Indian Proverb

An Indian proverb
with pearls of wisdom
in those sage eyes
they say she can
read your mind
there is strength in
her stride she catches
fire as graceful as a
gazelle twice she has
given birth to miracles
there is pleasure in the
plunge and only she can
fathom the depth of my love

The Victims Of Love

I read it in a book once
love is an illusion and
we are casualties of love
if in the aftermath
I am left paralyzed
seduced by the siren
hearing the sound of
my name from serene lips
being the victim of her love
maybe then it would all make sense

Figure Rene's

On top of the chest of drawers sits
a music box with a figurine of a ballerina
gracefully standing on her toes in pirouette
reaching for Heaven as her soft music caresses
me soothing my soul elegant and poised with a
calmness about her as she circles the room I am
spinning caught up in the balance the hips like
scales teetering back and forth from the weight
of all the curves that have been thrown her way
the strength in those legs keep reaching the thick
of it all I am lost in

Abuela

There is nothing more grand than
the children of sons the spitting image
breaking for smores after riding bicycles
in the cul de sac there are imperfections
at every turn splashing in puddles playing
with bubbles hearing their voices sing
abuela in praise memories of the house
so dear filling them with warmth cool to
the touch nurturing and nourishing she left
blessings in their room

Much A Thing As Beautiful Thunder

There is thunder
in Heaven tonight
when her touch
disappears I keep
running across her
like playing violin
the departure has
arrived beautifully
the sound

Hipnotic

The chime
announces
your presence
on the wind.
your royal
sashay
switching
and swaying
back and
forth like a
vessel sailing
through this
life moored
to this heart
bound there
by a love me
knot. everlasting
are your gifts.
you are the
fulfillment
of dreams

Mason Ajar

Mason is in
the cupboard
filled with
cookies his aunt
has gone away
to college dad
is under the
hood again
making the
plugs spark
he is such
a tool an action
figure in hand
flying through
the sky

Parables

Like the moths stalk the
sun so too is the dear
she speaks in parables
our children's children
are the interpretation
we are not seedless like
the watermelon or the
sunflower after it has been
relieved of its fruit
when the sermon is of love
watching her every move
they will speak Serene

LOVE

Apple Butter

Defying the
odds betting
against the
spread there
is a spooning
going on
so hands
are covered
in jam when
we are out
breaking bread
after the
caramelizing
comes the
buttering of buns

Fabric

She is forbidden in the haberdashery
for fear that she may shed her garments
wrap your arms around her mend and
hold her in high esteem this is a season
beyond measure she is my future and
sewn together my strength in her I am
vested fastened tailored for each other

Love Letter To The Rain

Dear
Lover
I am a
pluviophile
joyful
and
Serene
on days
filled
with
drops
of
you

Ascension

The fasten seat belt sign
came on and we came
undone. hope you're not
afraid of heights. there is
no flying under the radar.
embrace for impact. I will
celebrate you every day
even after we reach our
destination together. your
mother-in-law is in Heaven
at the Sandia Resort and Casino
and I plan to take you there

ATLANTIC CITY

Negotiate The Stairs

There was a door purchased to keep out the draught
beyond the door was a closet to keep in the skeletons
in the corner placed just so was a nook for the reading
a lamp to light the way a cupboard for all the seasons
stairs for elevation a table for the overflowing a roof
to keep in the heat and a window to watch the reign
a vanity for the beauty in the mirror image a threshold
was the bridge to cross as she built for us a home

Every Moment Of Forever

They don't know me
and even if I tried to
explain they would still
be clueless. don't want
to enter the ring like a
boxer. I am taking a knee.
here lies my proposal. Lets
cross the threshold like a
bridge to Heaven or fingers
crossing a harp making
beauty of the music

WINGS

Honey On The Causeway

There
was
an
eruption
and
like
Noah's
they
came
in two
now
a
path
paved
heading
my
way
sticky
and
wet
and
I
am
the
cause

On The Tip Of My Tongue

There are things
that have eluded me
some sink
without a trace but
I have never lost
sight of love
not even one memory
when I am tranquil
and calm
there is
peaceful elegance
upon my face
a name that
remains
Serene

10

Fire From The Hip

She was
born ready
for combat
in her boots
and fatigues
when she steps
out the door
she goes to war
like weapons
of mass destruction
when thrown
a curve deadly
the joint
current
powerfully
hipped
she is fire
you'll
discover
this is no
game
run for cover

The Pleasure Of Standing Still

Enjoying
the stillness
in the movement
standing fast
going no where
I'll stay right there
in motion less
and stationary
grounded
and when I come
unearthed
she stills
me

Solar Eclipse

I have been poverty stricken yet treasured
been enslaved and then captivated by a smile that set me free
once thought I had taken my last and she was a breath of fresh heir
in this hell her kisses have been the promise of Heaven
her hips speak to me raising me as if from the dead
like the smell of the coming rain I sense her coming
she melts the sun in full moon we eclipse
and I am being swept away by the wave

Just Shy Of Heaven

There is a Ferris wheel overlooking the harbor
filled with her screams then ice cream. on the
board walk she was a passenger in a boat to
nowhere and funnel cakes. just north of the south
hearts were in concert. across the border took
pleasure in being robbed by a one armed bandit.
passed up the reservation along the Rio Grande
in the land of enchantment. it was hoop dreams in
the mountains at state. did a ditty my girl in
motor town. off the boulevard dined on chicken
and waffles and mango's two stepped taking in serene
moments before a voyage to Atlantis setting spirits free
just shy of Heaven

Flowers For Rain

Sippin' Mother's Pink Champale out of Tupperware cups
left in the refrigerator after playing cards on the porch
seeing who was the fastest kid on the block as we raced
up the street then climbing the walls of the advocate before
it got dark because everyone was afraid to walk through
after dark climbing trees and catching lightning bugs trips
to Smith Playground, Wildwood and Hershey Park, playing
tops in the street and basketball on milk crates getting wet
running outside to take the flower patterned sheets from the
clothes lines as it started to rain. did you have flowers for rain?

In The Middle Of Serene Waters

My
heart
is an
island
safe
from
harm
there
is no
rescue
if left
stranded
everything
on this
island
is Serene

UNIROYAL
uniroyal.com

Contradiction

You don't stand a chance
for the encounter clockwise
even my lips are opposite yours
if you are holding yourself against me
I beg to differ if opposites attract then
you are my contradiction

Evolve

From a different angle
you were educated by the sea
like 360 degrees of separation
gradually yielding the evolution
of love came full circle and
then I heard you say
Ev love

The Compound

You are the keeper of the estate
you bartered for a place
south of Heaven
the last resort
you steadied the storm
with your
Serene intentions

You Turn

For us there was a layover
a delay in the motor city
there was no direct flight to love
afraid of reaching heights
when I noticed you take off
it was the kiss that made me soar

The Wet

We reside
among the
wet where
there is flood
warnings in
effect not to
be quenched
to bathe in
existence and
nothing else
to draw from

When I Consider Your Heavens

You have been
baptized in beauty
it pools at your feet
return to me even
if only in a dream
anoint me with
your Heavens

Thick

Your thighs
finely tuned like
a saxophone
they sing
a duet how
they keep
recurring in
my dreams
against walls
laced with lilies
leaving me thick
with submission

The Wrestle

You smell of
the coming rain
pouring surrender
you see in beautiful
your silence is loud
your waterfalls profound
you are not playing
a solo any more

Sweet After Taste

Your dreams
are delicious
filled with sugar
and vanilla chai tea
I want to have them
with desert

Riding The Wave

The sailor
and the wave
are inseparable
holding each other
like the night holds
the darkness like a bow
meets a curtsey like the
earth greets the sea

21st 2017

The Rhythm Of Rain

I will be your dreamcatcher
with bow and arrow for you I'd hunt
shelter you in the biggest teepee on the reservation
in smoke signals write you poems on the wind
beat the drums of war for you
if you'll dance to the rhythm of the rain

Firewater

How your love handles
it plays like music in the
foreground goes down
like firewater I have the
best seat in the house

There Is Nectar In Grafenberg

You are a season beyond measure
a temple and my heart dwells
in your chambers in you I rejoice
there is nectar in Grafenberg
come into my den and be devoured
let us love like gazelles among the lilies

Giving Berth To Love

Your lips are like lilies
dripping liquid myrrh
there is honey to be
drawn from your well
even your silhouette
is to be desired when
you give berth you
impregnate with love

Serene Highness

I am under your jurisdiction
there is refuge in your reign
you are towering from the fall
I am breathing you taking
in the gracious heir

The Sweetest Nectar

Your beauty is
for the harvesting
it is always your season
you are the sweetest nectar
there is nourishment in your touch

Ides Of July

There is
thick and
thievery
in your
stealth
of heart
in the
moments
stolen
abide with
me in the
ides of
July

The Deep Serene

I want to taste
the deep serene
I want to be the
reason you reason
to make you rise
then put you to sleep
you to salivate at the sound
of my name to be a floodgate
in the pouring rain to be your
poison and your antidote

Savior

There is severity in her kisses
she is committed to the caress
I am not disciplined enough to
avoid the flame she wraps her
arms around me and holds me
in high esteem

The Abduction

Being abducted
is not alien you
are July making
angels of the snow
like a butterfly you
do not yearn for the
fountain of youth only
to be cocooned

A Setting More Beautiful

Sitting under the blood orange sun
covered in blue from the berries. a
car broke down on the other side of
the Chesapeake Bay. the passenger
in a quest to prevent the sun from
melting like most men, not shelter,
for shade took refuge in the suitor.
more radiant than a thousand suns.
more beautiful than a thousand
settings. as the shadows began to
disappear into the darkness the make
of the car will never be remembered
in her setting.

A Prayer Made For Two

There is no plateau
riding solo in a prayer
made for two so I
pushed aside the pillow
and met her at the arch
where the heel and the
ball valleys just below
the baby toe planting
kisses in the bed of
flowered pajamas

Chaise

This is not catch
and release or cat
and mouse lets chaise
smother me in your
kisses until I turn a
yellow shade of blue

Current

There is liquid in
your movement
you are current
I see you clear like
the waters of the
Providenciales
the way you flow
upstream sweeping
me away

Watching Love

You think no
one sees you
but you can't
hide your
beauty there
are eyes
watching
even when
you are not
looking
when you
don't want
to be seen
sometimes
you are
invisible I
see you then

Pardon My French Kiss

The queen
in the white
castle listening
to the prince
telling her
how much
she is adored
her crown
rests among
the foundations
when she walks
her fingers across
my chest she
pardons my
French kiss

To you I turn
you give me
direction you
are the global
positon of my
heart I adore
nothing more
than the landscape
of you

Setting Fires

The
evening
brushed
against
her thigh
like
molasses
for cookies
this tall glass
of elegance
most days
she caresses
the sun there
is passion
in the burn
a thing of
beauty
if you're
digesting
the flame

The Surrender

There is
wisdom
in your
resistance
wear it like
a badge of
honor your
misdemeanor
yours is
delicious
for breakfast
in full moon
I am covered
in your honey
and surrender

How We Pillow Fight

She
pushes
aside
the
pillow
talk
and
begins
to
smother
me
with
kiss
after
kiss

The Beauty Of Love In Beast Mode

Some things
remain the
same even
in the midst
of change
in mode
there is a
constant I
am a creature
of beastly
habit always
loving her
thing of beauty

CPSIA information can be obtained
at www.ICGtesting.com
Printed in the USA
BVHW03*1007290618
520434BV00004B/19/P